The

QBQ!

WORKBOOK

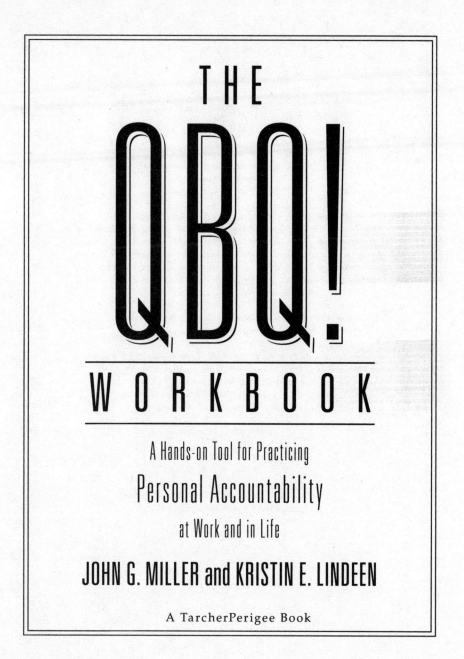

THE
QBQ!
WORKBOOK

A Hands-on Tool for Practicing
Personal Accountability
at Work and in Life

JOHN G. MILLER and KRISTIN E. LINDEEN

A TarcherPerigee Book

tarcherperigee

An imprint of Penguin Random House LLC
375 Hudson Street
New York, New York 10014

Most TarcherPerigee books are available at special quantity discounts
for bulk purchase for sales promotions, premiums, fund-raising,
and educational needs. Special books or book excerpts also
can be created to fit specific needs. For details, write:
SpecialMarkets@penguinrandomhouse.com.

ISBN: 9780143129912

Printed in the United States of America
1   3   5   7   9   10   8   6   4   2

Welcome to *The QBQ! Workbook* . . .

—[QBQ!]—

The purpose of this workbook is to encourage true learning beyond reading *QBQ! The Question Behind the Question*®. In a nutshell, the QBQ® is a tool that helps each individual ask better questions so that he or she can practice **personal accountability** in all areas of life. This *QBQ! Workbook* was inspired by the book *QBQ!*® and the principles taught in it. It is our hope that you will read the *QBQ!* book and then work through this study guide as a means to better absorb and apply the life-changing content in *QBQ!* More than a fad, slogan, or catchphrase, the QBQ is a tool that can sharpen our focus, reenergize our tired routines, and lead to bold improvements in work and life.

As is written in *QBQ!*, learning equals change. If one has not *changed*, one has not truly *learned*. Meaningful change occurs when we think more deeply, reflect more personally, engage with content more frequently—all leading to action. Only when true, accountable personal study takes place can the ideas and methods in *QBQ!* leap from the page straight into our lives. It's then that the QBQ becomes part of our daily walk. When **personal accountability** becomes a core and guiding value in a person's life, great things happen!

At QBQ, Inc., we exist to help *you*, the *QBQ!* reader and learner, as well as our customer, apply the *QBQ!* material at work and home. So, please, never hesitate to reach out to us at QBQ.com.

Thank you for believing in the powerful principle of **personal accountability!**

JOHN G. MILLER
Author of QBQ!
John@QBQ.com

KRISTIN E. LINDEEN
COO, QBQ, Inc.
Kristin@QBQ.com

Introduction

—[QBQ!]—

What Ever Happened to . . .

A billboard reads, "What ever happened to personal responsibility?" All around us we see examples of people passing the buck—saying things like "It's not my department!" and "Who dropped the ball?" While this type of response is sometimes understandable, it doesn't do anything to solve the problem. There's a better way.

Key Takeaway:

Personal accountability is needed everywhere.

---

1. Personal responsibility: Write down three words that come to mind when you think of the concept of personal responsibility:

   _____

   _____

   _____

2. These questions are all commonly heard examples of a lack of personal accountability:

   "When is that department going to do its job?"
   "Why don't they communicate better?"
   "Who dropped the ball?"
   "Why do we have to go through all this change?"
   "When is someone going to train me?"
   "Why can't we find better people?"
   "Who's going to give us a clear vision?"

   Put an asterisk next to those you've heard before. Put a check mark next to the questions you've asked yourself before. Can you add any more questions that indicate a lack of personal responsibility?

   _____

   _____

   _____

3. Which statement is most true for you? Circle one.

I think I am pretty accountable, but anyone can improve!

I'm not entirely sure what is meant by "accountable" yet.

When it comes to being accountable, I have good and bad moments.

I'm not accountable, and it's everyone else's fault!

Somebody gave me *QBQ!* to read, and I was offended!

CHAPTER ONE

A Picture of Personal Accountability

QBQ!

An overworked young waiter goes above and beyond to deliver good service to a customer and pays for it out of pocket, too. Instead of shrugging off the situation by saying, "We don't serve Diet Coke," he goes the extra mile to get one across the street. This decision to solve the problem, made in the moment, makes all the difference.

Key Takeaway:

Personal accountability turns a moment of frustration into an opportunity to contribute.

1. Jacob's story makes you feel:

   ❏ energized   ❏ frustration
   ❏ encouraged   ❏ a desire to change
   ❏ disbelief   ❏ a craving for Diet Coke
   ❏ relief

   Summarize in one sentence your No. 1 takeaway from Jacob's story.

   _____

   _____

   _____

2. If you had been Jacob, would you have stopped to serve the customer or kept on going to the kitchen? Why or why not?

   _____

   _____

   _____

3. Underline in the QBQ definition below the words that are meaningful to you. The definition of the QBQ:

   A tool that enables individuals to practice personal accountability by making better choices in the moment.

4. If personal accountability is about "making better choices," identify two good choices you've made lately and two lousy ones.

_____

_____

_____

5. The "Jacob and the Diet Coke" story is a metaphor for going the "extra mile" for another person. Think about whom you can get a "Diet Coke" for. Ask yourself the QBQ, "What can I do to serve

_____?" (Fill in that person's name.)

The last time I had outstanding service like this was at

_____.

Having someone go the extra mile for me makes me feel

_____.

6. What makes one person more accountable than another? Circle
   the things below that you believe drive individuals to be more
   accountable:

   upbringing   desire to win/compete

   life experiences   energy

   self-discipline   thinking

   Which one or two do you need to work on in your life so you

   can practice more personal accountability? _____

   _____

CHAPTER TWO

Making Better Choices

QBQ!

Goatheads are prickly little thorns that grow in the prairie lands and stick to our shoes and pop bike tires. They are a metaphor for incorrect thinking like "I have to" or "I can't." These statements can stick in our minds and cause problems. Making the better choice to focus on good thoughts is key to practicing personal accountability.

> **Key Takeaway:**
>
> **Personal accountability is practiced by making better choices.**

1. I have good control over my thoughts. True or false? (circle one)

2. Consider a time when you made a poor choice and landed in a "field of goatheads." Were you able to recover and get back on track? If so, how? What did you learn from the experience?

_____

_____

_____

3. Reflect on this idea: Even deciding *not* to choose is making a choice. Think of something you decided *not* to do recently. Was it a good or bad decision?

_____

_____

_____

4. Fill in the blank: People who believe they have no choice say things such as the following:

I _____ to.

I _____.

5. Use this exercise to challenge yourself and think through your beliefs about the choices you have in life.

Choices and Consequences exercise:

I HAVE to do the laundry. True or false? (circle one)

(Do you really *have* to?)

Consequence of not doing the laundry:

_____

(There is freedom in realizing I don't have to do it, but "get" to or "choose" to because I don't like the alternative—dirty clothes!)

I HAVE to pay my taxes. True or false?

Consequence of not paying taxes:

_____

I HAVE to go to work. True or false?

Consequence of not going to work:

_____

Create your own "HAVE to" statement:

_____

Consequence: _____

I CAN'T exercise consistently.

TRUTH: I have not created time in my schedule and could choose to make space for regular exercise.

I CAN'T improve my relationships.

TRUTH: _____

I CAN'T share my true feelings.

TRUTH: _____

Create your own "CAN'T" statement:

_____

Rewrite and replace the "HAVE to's" and "CAN'Ts" in your statements with "CHOOSE to's" and "CANs."

_____

_____

_____

How does that change how you feel when you read your statements?

When I use the phrase "I can't," I feel _____.

When I use the phrase "I choose," I feel _____.

6. Summary of chapters 1 and 2:

Personal accountability is the essence of QBQ, which is

making better _____ in the moment by

asking better _____. (fill in the blanks)

CHAPTER THREE

QBQ! The Question Behind the Question

—|QBQ!|—

The *QBQ!* book is all about choosing to ask better questions, and the QBQ is always a better question. QBQs begin with "What" or "How," contain an "I," and focus on "action." Ask these better questions and begin to get better answers!

> **Key Takeaway:**
>
> **How to create the question behind the question—the QBQ.**

1. Fill in the blank: Better questions lead to better _____.

2. Underline the "better" questions:

   "When are we going to solve that problem?"

   "How can I adapt to this change?"

"Who didn't get me that information on time?"

"What improvements can I make?"

Looking at the "better" questions you underlined, circle the pieces that match the three guidelines listed in the book.

QBQ Guidelines

QBQs . . .

1. Begin with "What" or "How"
2. Contain an "I"
3. Focus on "Action"

3. Fill in the blanks:

QBQs . . .

Begin with "_____" or "_____."

Contain an "_____."

Focus on "_____."

QBQs do NOT start with "_____," "When," or "_____."

QBQs do NOT contain the words "_____," "_____,"

or "_____"

4. To be clear, QBQs are generally asked of whom?

   Answer: _____.

5. Let's take a quiz to determine which lousy questions you are most tempted to ask. Choose one answer for each of the scenarios below. Just have fun with it, and you can tally your "score" at the end.

   1. You just found out you have to take a really difficult test for a certification at work that you didn't think you had to have. Which question below might you ask yourself?

      • Why didn't anyone clarify for me that I needed this?
      ▲ When will they update the standards?
      ■ Who was supposed to help me prepare?

   2. You can't decide if you should quit your job and take a risk with a new venture or if you should play it safe and stay where you are. Your spouse doesn't have any opinion either way. What question would you ask?

      • Why doesn't s/he care about this decision?
      ■ Who got me stuck at this point in life?
      ▲ When will someone just tell me what choice to make?

   3. You don't like your manager at your job. After a frustrating day when you were yelled at for being late, how do you respond?

- Why is life so unfair?
- Who does this guy think he is, anyway?
- When will someone get me up on time?

4. Last week you forgot to take the garbage cans out to the curb, and your spouse got mad. What question might you ask yourself?

   - When will my husband/wife lay off me?
   - Who is going to remind me to take out the trash from now on?
   - Why do I have to do all the work?

5. Your kids are begging for the next hot device. You just bought them one recently, but they're already bored with it. What question do you find yourself asking?

   - Who created these devices anyway?
   - Why are my children so demanding?
   - When are my kids going to be more grateful?

6. You're overwhelmed thinking about finances and the future. How do you frame your thoughts on this?

   - When is my financial adviser going to give me more guidance?
   - Why is college so expensive?
   - Who got me into all this debt?

7. One of your closest friends hasn't been speaking to you lately. You know he is mad at you, but you're not sure why. How do you think about this conflict?

   ■ Who caused this problem in the first place?
   ● Why are my friends so hard to get along with?
   ▲ When am I going to find better friends who don't take so much work?

8. You've heard that someone said something about you behind your back. The rumor is spreading quickly, and you're not sure how to stop it. What do you ask?

   ▲ When is someone else going to stand up for me and shut this rumor down?
   ● Why are other people so mean?
   ■ Who's doing this to me?

9. You didn't get the promotion you applied for last year, but you worked really hard and improved during the past twelve months. You're the senior employee, and you think you've got a shot at this position. The announcement is made . . . and someone who's worked there less time got the job. How do you respond?

   ■ Who influenced the boss to side against me?
   ● Why don't I get what I deserve?
   ▲ When will I catch a break?

10. Your significant other has been distant lately. You've tried hard to reach out and connect but can't figure out how to bridge the gap. What thoughts do you have about this?

    ■ Who's going to fix this?
    ▲ When will s/he recognize that I'm trying my hardest?
    ● Why are relationships so hard?

Add up your answers.

How many ■ questions did you choose? _____

How many ▲ questions did you choose? _____

How many ● questions did you choose? _____

KEY: ■ = "Blame" questions.
        ▲ = "Procrastination" questions.
        ● = "Complaining" or "Victim Thinking" questions.

The shape with the largest number just might be the "trap"

that you struggle with most. According to this quiz, my biggest

struggle is _____.

CALL TO ACTION

What is the most important idea for me to apply from the introduction through chapter 3?

_____

_____

_____

What steps will I take to make this change? When will I start? Be as specific as possible.

_____

_____

_____

How will my life improve by taking this action?

_____

_____

_____

CHAPTER FOUR

Don't Ask "Why?"

QBQ!

Questions that begin with "Why" instead of "What" or "How" are lousy questions because they cause feelings of powerlessness. "Why me?" questions lead to victim thinking, which is a dangerous place to live. Want victim thinking eliminated from society? Then, as individuals, we must first eliminate it from ourselves.

> **Key Takeaway:**
>
> **Asking "Why" questions leads to victim thinking.**

1. These four "Why" questions are given as examples of poor questions:

   "Why don't others work harder?"
   "Why is this happening to me?"
   "Why do they make it so difficult for me to do my job?"
   "Why don't people care as much as I do?"

   Write out two of the above questions that you are most at risk of asking.

   "Why _____?"

   "Why _____?"

2. List those things you whine about frequently. Example: "I whine about people not being friendlier."

   I whine about _____.

   I whine about _____.

   I whine about _____.

   I whine about _____.

   I tend to play the victim when I feel (circle all that apply):

   defensive   discouraged

   caught off guard   sad

   angry   aggravated

   out of control   hurt

Others:

_____

_____

_____

3. List some "Why" questions that you've been asking that have led you to play the victim, whine, and complain:

_____

_____

_____

4. What if our world had absolutely NO victim thinking, whining, or complaining? What would be different? The same? Better? Worse?

_____

_____

_____

5. The best way to get rid of victim thinking in our world and society is to start with eliminating it in ourselves. What steps can you take to eliminate victim thinking in your life?

_____

_____

_____

There are three "better" questions—QBQs—listed below as alternatives to the "Why" questions that lead to victim thinking.

"How can I do my job better today?"
"What can I do to improve the situation?"
"How can I support others?"

Create your own below.

"How _____?"

"What _____?"

"How _____?"

" _____?"

" _____?"

CHAPTER FIVE

The Victim

—QBQ!—

Years after returning to civilian life, a military man, once trained in the "no excuses" lifestyle of military service, realized he had fallen into the trap of victim thinking. Recognizing the series of "Why" questions he had been asking, he realized he'd become what he disliked most: *the victim.* A "no excuses" lifestyle is a better way to live.

Key Takeaway:

"No excuses" thinking beats
victim thinking.

1. Why is it so easy for people to slip into excuse-making mode? List your thoughts/reasons:

   _____

   _____

   _____

2. How does a "no excuses" attitude lead to greater personal accountability?

   _____

   _____

   _____

3. List three excuses you hear others use:

   _____

   _____

   _____

   List three excuses you use:

   _____

   _____

   _____

4. Finish this statement: I slip into excuse-making mode when I feel

_____

5. List the benefits eliminating excuses from your life would provide:

_____

_____

_____

CHAPTER SIX

"Why Is This Happening to Me?"

—[QBQ!]—

A reader of *QBQ!* believed she could disprove the idea that "stress is a choice." Thirty days later, she admitted that stress *is* a choice! Bad things happen, unexpected circumstances arise, but so often "stress" is mostly about how a person chooses to respond.

> **Key Takeaway:**
>
> **Stress is a choice.**

1. Stress is a choice. Agree or disagree?

   _____

2. What typically "stresses you out"? What "triggers" you to choose stress?

   _____

   _____

   _____

3. In reviewing the trigger events that led you to choose stress in your life—could you have made better choices? If so, how?

_____

_____

_____

4. Explain how embracing the idea that stress is a choice would enhance your daily living.

_____

_____

_____

5. It's important to recognize where stress and tension begin. Yes, bad things happen, and life can be hard, but so often it's the individual's response that creates increased levels of stress. Will you commit to owning the concept that "I create my own stress!"? Circle Yes or No . . . it's always a choice! Reflect on this concept, and your response of yes or no.

_____

_____

_____

CHAPTER SEVEN

"Why Do We Have to Go Through All This Change?"

—[QBQ!]—

A pilot and his young daughter Stacey took a plane out for a spin one afternoon. When complications arose, the engine quit working. Instead of asking lousy questions and complaining about the situation, the pilot asked good questions, took action, and solved the problem. (And saved the day!) When one is faced with change and challenging situations, it's better to act than to resist. Fighting change is rarely worth the effort. Instead, ask the QBQ "How can I adapt?"

Key Takeaway:

The QBQ enables us to change.

1. Change makes me feel (check all that apply)

    ❏ empowered   ❏ anxious
    ❏ exhilarated   ❏ apprehensive
    ❏ empty   ❏ paralyzed
    ❏ energized   ❏ powerful

2. What changes are you dealing with right now? Are you fighting or adapting?

Change: _____

_____. Fighting or adapting? (Circle one.)

Change: _____

_____. Fighting or adapting? (Circle one.)

Change: _____

_____. Fighting or adapting? (Circle one.)

3. Underline the QBQs that would be most effective for you when facing change:

"What can I do to improve?"

"How can I adapt?"

"What can I do to better understand?"

"How can I communicate more clearly?"

"What can I do to grow?"

"What changes can I make to prepare for more change?"

4. Case Study

Matthew was working at a company that was acquired by a
larger, more "corporate" organization. Matthew's employer was
more of a mom-and-pop-type shop, but all that was going to
change. As the changes started coming, Matthew found it difficult to focus on the positives. The whole culture at the office
started to shift. People were let go; new people were brought in.
Headquarters was now located across the country; it felt as if everything was changing. Matthew and his co-workers—those
who were left—often huddled around, asking questions like
"Why do we have to go through all this change?" "When are
things going to settle down?" "Why have we lost the 'family
feel'?" "Who thought this change in leadership was a good idea?"
"Why didn't they ask our opinions before taking this path?"

- What could Matthew change about his behavior that would
  result in a more positive work experience?

_____

_____

- Come up with three QBQs Matthew could ask instead of
  the lousy questions listed above and write them below.

_____

_____

_____

5. Stacey's dad, of course, was physically in the cockpit. But being "in the cockpit" also serves as a metaphor. He could have whined and complained about forces beyond his control, yet he didn't seem to. He simply recognized he was in control of his own thoughts and actions and proceeded to own the problem. How about you? The last time you were hit with tremendous forces of change, how did you respond? Knowing the QBQ now, how would you handle it all differently? Explain.

CHAPTER EIGHT

"Why Don't They Communicate Better?"

—QBQ!—

Communication is a two-way street. It takes a lot of work to communicate effectively! Asking "Why don't they communicate better?" is an ineffective way to deal with communication difficulties. A QBQ such as "How can I better understand others?" guides us along the path of enhanced communication.

> ### Key Takeaway:
>
> **Communication is about understanding the other person.**

1. Do you consider yourself a good communicator? Circle Yes or No. Why or why not?

_____

_____

_____

2. When I feel misunderstood, I (check all that apply)

❑ get angry
❑ try harder
❑ feel sad
❑ try sign language
❑ examine my
   communication style
❑ withdraw
❑ watch TV

❑ talk to someone else
   about it
❑ give up
❑ think about how I can
   improve
❑ _____
❑ _____
❑ _____

3. Have you ever found yourself saying, "Why doesn't anyone understand me?" or "Why won't my _____ (kids, spouse, friends, boss) listen to me?" List five to ten costs of asking these questions.

_____

_____

_____

_____

_____

4. Communication is a two-way street. It's sending and receiving messages. Where do you need more improvement: In the sending of your message (making sure your communication to the other person is clear) or in the receiving of others' messages (making sure you are receiving their communication as they intended it—that is, listening well)?

_____

_____

_____

5. How are accountability and communication related?

_____

_____

_____

6. Chapter 8 closes with two QBQs . . . underline the one you will commit to using today!

"What can I do to become a more effective listener?"

"How can I better understand others?"

Or . . . both!

What relationship can I improve immediately by asking either or both of those QBQs? What rewards will come from making this specific relationship better?

Reflect for a few minutes, and write out your thoughts below.

_____

_____

_____

_____

_____

CALL TO ACTION

What is the most important idea for me to apply from chapters 4–8?

_____

_____

_____

What steps will I take to make this change? When will I start? Be as specific as possible.

_____

_____

_____

How will my life improve by taking this action?

_____

_____

_____

CHAPTER NINE

Don't Ask "When?"

—QBQ!—

Procrastination has many consequences. Questions that begin with "When" lead to procrastination. A little delay here, a little postponing there, and soon there's a serious problem. The solution to these "When" questions is to ask QBQs, like "How can I contribute right now?" and "What can I do to take action?"

Key Takeaway:

"When" questions lead us to procrastination.

1. Procrastination is (check all that apply)

❏ just a part of life
❏ something typical of lazy people
❏ no harm to anyone

❏ something I try hard to avoid
❏ a bad habit I've conquered

2. I procrastinate most on

_____

_____

_____

The costs of procrastinating on this are

_____

_____

_____

3. I tend to procrastinate when I (check all that apply)

❑ feel scared
❑ think I can't do something
❑ don't want to do something
❑ feel overwhelmed
❑ have to work with other people

❑ think something's not important
❑ feel as if I can't make a difference
❑ am not sure how to move forward
❑ want to sleep instead

4. In the space below jot down the "When" questions you tend to ask from this list.

   "When will they take care of the problem?"

   "When will the customer call me back?"

   "When will we get the information we need to make a decision?"

   "When will they tell us what's going on?"

   _____

   _____

   _____

5. What "When" questions that lead to procrastination, paralysis, and inaction can you add?

   _____

   _____

   _____

6. The guidelines for building a QBQ are (1) begin with "What" or "How," (2) contain an "I," and (3) focus on "Action." Create procrastination-defeating QBQs in the space below, such as:

"What solution can I provide?"

"How can I more creatively reach my customer?"

"What can I do to find the information I need to make a decision?"

"How can I excel in my work right now?"

_____

_____

_____

7. Does your organization have the speed required to be outstanding? What could improve how fast the organization moves?

_____

_____

_____

8. Fill in the blank on this critical point: Remember, the answers

are in the _____.

9. What specific action will you now take "before lunch"?

_____

_____

_____

CHAPTER TEN

Procrastination: The Friend of Failure

—[QBQ!]—

A father left a large piece of glass leaning against a basketball pole on the driveway. He thought to himself, "I'll put it away later." All day long he told himself, "I'll do it later!" That evening, his son was completing a chore and ran right into and through the large piece of glass. *I'll do it later!* thinking is costly in many ways.

Key Takeaway:

Take care of the little things while they're still little.

1. "Take care of the little things while they're still little." Write any examples you have of this statement being valid.

   _____

   _____

   _____

2. How did the story of Michael running through the glass make you feel? Does it cause you to want to take any specific action right now? If so, what is it?

_____

_____

_____

3. Is there anything you're saying "I'll do it later!" to in life? Visualize the long-term consequences of continuing to put off action. What thoughts come to mind?

_____

_____

_____

4. What is the first step to take toward taking care of that "little thing" you've been saying "I'll do it later" to? Be specific.

_____

_____

_____

5. Fill in the blank:

"Procrastination is the friend of _____."

CHAPTER ELEVEN

"When Will We Get More Tools and Better Systems?"

—[QBQ!]—

Creativity is an essential component of success. Focusing on what is lacking on the job leads to procrastination, victim thinking, and blame, all of which hinder creativity. Learn to succeed "within the box" by asking, "How can I achieve with the resources I already have?"

> **Key Takeaway:**
>
> **True creativity is succeeding with the tools and resources I already have.**

1. In your own words, define creativity.

_____

_____

_____

2. It's often said that creativity is thinking outside the box. How is that different from believing that creativity is succeeding within the box?

_____

_____

_____

3. Chart your decision-making process in the space below. Ask yourself, "What do I need to have in order to make a decision?" "What steps do I take?"

Example:

Step 1: Gather information
Step 2: Call my mom
Step 3: Set it aside and watch TV
Step 4: Survey a dozen friends
Step 5: Decide!

_____

_____

_____

_____

4. Are you a decisive person? Explain.

_____

_____

_____

5. Write down three decisions that you need to make this year.

1. _____

2. _____

3. _____

6. What resources do you feel you are lacking?

_____

_____

_____

7. "I find that every time I do the job with the tools I have, I tend to receive more tools." —Deb Weber of State Farm Insurance

   Do you find this statement to be true or false where you work? How so, or how not?

   _____

   _____

   _____

8. How can the QBQ "How can I achieve with the resources I already have?" lead to increased creativity, for you personally?

   _____

   _____

   _____

CHAPTER TWELVE

"When Are We Going to Hear Something New?"

———[QBQ!]———

The principle of personal accountability is timeless; it's a fundamental idea that never grows old. It always applies. As do many other timeless ideas. Asking "When are we going to hear something new?" is not an accountable question. Instead, asking "How can I apply what I'm hearing?" promotes true learning and personal growth. The old stuff IS the good stuff!

Key Takeaway:

**It's not about hearing;
it's about applying.**

1. There are several fundamentals for effective selling. Getting up early, contacting prospective clients, sharing belief in the products and services being sold, and of course following up with customers. No matter what your profession or role is, what are some fundamentals required for success?

_____

_____

_____

2. "How can I apply what I'm hearing?" is a tremendous question to ask oneself. Where in your life do you need to employ that QBQ today?

_____

_____

_____

3. Cynicism is defined as "doubting another's intentions, sincerity, or good will." Rejecting ideas because you've heard them before is a form of cynicism.

   Ask and answer the question "Am I a cynical person?" Explain your thoughts, and record examples here:

   _____

   _____

   _____

4. The old stuff is the good stuff! Many important ideas are not "timely" but rather "timeless."

   Here are some "old" principles. Put an X next to the ones you'd like to spend some time reflecting on or working to improve on.

   _____ Spending less than I make helps me stay financially secure.

   _____ Exercising regularly is good for my heart and waistline.

   _____ Eating fruits and vegetables is a healthier choice than eating donuts and chips.

   _____ Making eye contact with the person talking to me is the polite thing to do.

   _____ "No excuses!" living is a better way to live than blaming and finger-pointing.

   _____ Showing interest in others is a better approach than always talking about myself.

CALL TO ACTION

What is the most important idea for me to apply from chapters 9–12?

_____

_____

_____

What steps will I take to make this change? When will I start? Be as specific as possible.

_____

_____

_____

How will my life improve by taking this action?

_____

_____

_____

CHAPTER THIRTEEN

Don't Ask "Who?"

—⟨QBQ!⟩—

Blame and "whodunit" questions solve nothing and actually create more problems. A van driver explained the cycle of blame in his company, and there were only twelve employees! No matter the size of the organization or group of people, blame is costly. Blame is present when questions are asked beginning with "Who."

Key Takeaway:

"Whodunit" questions lead
to blame, and blame is costly.

The Company Coat of Arms

1. In any group of people, there tends to be a "circle of blame." This person blames this person, who points the finger at that person, who throws up her arms and yells, "It's all YOUR fault!" And the cycle goes on and on and on. Identify the "Circle of Blame" in your world. (It might not be an exact circle!) Draw it below.

2. There are consequences when we allow the blaming and finger-pointing to run rampant. For example, we miss out on good things when we're busy casting blame. List as many "costs" of blame as you are able to brainstorm.

_____

_____

_____

3. Name a relationship in your life that's been damaged by blame:

_____

Identify three ways blame has hurt this relationship.

1. _____

2. _____

3. _____

Reflect on the role you've played in this situation, and consider how you could begin the process of healing. Journal your thoughts below.

_____

_____

_____

_____

_____

_____

4. Where you work, is the culture one of brainstorming or "blame-storming"? Explain.

_____

_____

_____

5. Consider a current situation in your life right now where it would be easy to cast blame. Answer the QBQs:

"What can I do today to solve the problem?"

Answer:_____

"How can I help move the project forward?"

Answer:_____

"What action can I take to 'own' the situation?"

Answer:_____

Create your own QBQ:

_____

Answer:_____

Create your own QBQ:

_____

Answer:_____

CHAPTER FOURTEEN

A Poor Sailor Blames the Wind

—QBQ!—

The key to becoming an accountable person is eliminating all blame—even resisting the urge to blame oneself. Accountable people don't lay blame anywhere. Instead, they seek solutions and look to the future by learning from mistakes.

> ## Key Takeaway:
>
> **Accountable people look for solutions, not scapegoats.**

1. Fill in the blanks:

A poor teacher blames the _____.

A poor salesperson blames the _____.

A poor parent blames the _____.

A poor manager blames the _____.

A poor employee blames the _____.

A poor coach blames the _____.

Can you come up with a few more? List them below.

A poor _____ blames the _____.

A poor _____ blames the _____.

A poor _____ blames the _____.

2. Fill in the blank:

   Whom do accountable people blame? _____.

   Not even _____.

3. When a self-critique is warranted, how does it differ from self-blame?

   _____

   _____

   _____

4. Think of a mistake you made recently. Answer these two QBQs:

"What could I have done differently?"

_____

_____

_____

"How can I learn from this experience?"

_____

_____

_____

CHAPTER FIFTEEN

Silos

QBQ!

A vice president of operations jested, "We don't have any 'we/they' syndrome here, but it is 'us against them!'" There's little personal accountability in an environment with silos and infighting. Whether at work or at home, it's important to remember that everyone is on the same team.

> ### Key Takeaway:
>
> **We're all on the same team.**

1. A "silo" is typically a vertical structure used in farming to house grain and other material. In the organizational world, silos are usually different departments that do not share the same priorities, experience little communication between them, and sometimes operate as individual business units or entities within the same enterprise. Identify an organization you're involved with, in your professional or personal life, and list the "silos" present in that organization.

_____

_____

_____

2. Do you ever say or hear the phrase "It's not my job"? If so, in regards to what?

_____

_____

_____

3. Who's on your "team" in life? List the names of people who are teammates with you—people whom you couldn't succeed at work or at home without.

_____

_____

_____

4. Circle the words that resonate with you when you think of working on a team. Then list a few of your own.

helpful   frustrating

difficult   pointless

mind-blowing   productive

energizing   purposeful

energy draining   necessary

_____

5. Do you have experience with "we/they" and "us versus them"? How did it feel to work in that environment? Were there any attempts made—by you or anyone else—to break down the silos?

_____

_____

_____

6. Create three QBQs that strengthen teams.

   Example: "What can I do today to support the team's goal?"

   _____

   _____

   _____

7. Silos and infighting create an environment where it's like being on a tandem bike with all the riders facing different direc-
   tions. It's draining and exhausting. Use the tandem bike
   analogy and tie it to a situation you've been involved with in
   your life. What happens when people work against each other?

   _____

   _____

   _____

8. If you've been hunkered down in any kind of silo, what will
   you do today to climb out of it? What will be the value in doing
   so?

   _____

   _____

   _____

CHAPTER SIXTEEN

Beat the Ref

—| QBQ! |—

Athletes have three people to beat in every competition: their opponent, themselves, and the official. "Beating the ref" is a metaphor for both overcoming and letting go of what we cannot control. Instead of asking lousy questions that begin with "Why," "When," or "Who" and falling into the traps of victim thinking, procrastination, and blame, one must learn to be good enough to beat the ref by asking The Ultimate QBQ, "How can I let go of what I can't control?"

Key Takeaway:

To win in life,
I must focus on what I can control.

1. What does "good enough to beat the ref" mean to you? Put it in
   your own words.

   _____

   _____

   _____

2. The "beat the ref" metaphor is about letting go of what we
   cannot control. So, who or what is the "ref" in your life right
   now?

   _____

3. What will be the value to you in letting go?

   _____

   _____

   _____

4. What person or problem beyond your control is standing between you and success? List some barriers—people or
   problems—in your life.

   _____

   _____

   _____

5. Now, rather than focusing on these barriers, you need to focus on what you can control—*yourself.* Look at your list and ask the QBQ "What can *I* do to make a change?" and then write out what you will do differently.

_____

_____

_____

6. Create three QBQs to aid in this process of "beating the ref." Use the three QBQ guidelines: (1) Begins with "What" or "How," (2) contains an "I," (3) focuses on "action."

_____

_____

_____

CHAPTER SEVENTEEN

"Who Dropped the Ball?"

—| QBQ! |—

A flight attendant avoided the temptation to complain and blame and instead made the best of a bad situation. She left a lasting and positive impression on her customers. Personal accountability happens when we make better choices.

> ## Key Takeaway:
>
> **Personal accountability changes the world, one choice at a time.**

Bonita's story: A flight was delayed and stuck on the tarmac. The tension was high, and the passengers were unhappy. One flight attendant chose to make a difference. Instead of asking "Why did they overbook the plane?" or "Who dropped the ball?" she asked, "What can I do right now to make a difference?" And she handed out headphones for free while wearing a Santa Claus hat to bring smiles to everyone's face. That's how one person choosing personal accountability can make a lasting impact.

1. Reread the Bonita story and fill in the blanks: Instead of "Why

   did they _____ the plane?" or "Who dropped the

   _____?" The better question is "What can

   _____ do right now to make a _____?"

2. Reflect on Bonita's story. What did she do that made a difference that you would like to emulate?

   _____

   _____

   _____

3. A "Bonita Moment" is defined as when someone has dropped the ball, tension is high, mistakes have been made, and the customer is unhappy. Describe your last "Bonita Moment" in detail and how you responded.

_____

_____

_____

Now that you know the QBQ, how would you respond differently?

_____

_____

_____

4. Have you ever been in a situation where you were not at fault but had the opportunity to solve the problem or make a difference? How did you handle yourself in that moment?

_____

_____

_____

5. Fill in the blank: That's how personal accountability changes the world: one _____ at a time.

CHAPTER EIGHTEEN

Ownership

—[QBQ!]—

The third repairman arrived to attempt to fix a residential phone line. The first two had tried and failed. After surveying the problem and the work performed by the other repair people, he didn't lay blame or make excuses. Instead, he simply said, "I can't explain it, but I sure can apologize for it and see what I can do to solve your problem!" Ownership is the solution to blame and makes all the difference.

Key Takeaway:

Ownership is personal accountability in its purest form.

1. Write down words that come to mind when you hear the term "ownership."

   _____

   _____

   _____

2. What was in the phone company repairman's approach that you could emulate immediately?

   _____

   _____

   _____

3. Fill in the blank: Ownership: "A commitment of the _____,

   heart, and _____ to fix the _____ and

   never again affix the _____." How would your life change if you made that commitment? Reflect and write your thoughts below.

   _____

   _____

   _____

4. Create two QBQs that would help you take more ownership and cast less blame. Example: "What can I do to accept responsibility for the problem?"

_____

_____

_____

5. Describe a problem or difficult situation in your life. How would asking the two QBQs you created improve it? What is your plan to tackle this problem now?

_____

_____

_____

_____

_____

Note: To gain a greater understanding of the powerful principle of **ownership,** read *Flipping the Switch: Unleash the Power of Personal Accountability Using the QBQ!* by John G. Miller.

CALL TO ACTION

What is the most important idea for me to apply from chapters 13–18?

_____

_____

_____

What steps will I take to make this change? When will I start? Be as specific as possible.

_____

_____

_____

How will my life improve by taking this action?

_____

_____

_____

CHAPTER NINETEEN

The Foundation of Teamwork

QBQ!

The differences between a dolphin and a giraffe are easy to spot—and appreciate. Likewise, true teammates view each other's strengths and the differences between them as beneficial and a source of value. A team is stronger when the individuals accept each other and enjoy the view.

Key Takeaway:

**Teams are stronger when people
are appreciated just the way they are.**

1. Write down the names of two or three people who frustrate you.

_____

_____

_____

How would you explain why that person grates on your nerves? Example: Harry—talks too much, is too opinionated.

_____

_____

_____

Look at the characteristics you've listed for that person, and rewrite them as a strength. Example: Harry—loves to connect with people, has lots of ideas.

_____

_____

_____

2. Just as we wouldn't expect a dolphin to stretch its neck like a giraffe, we must learn to see and appreciate people's differences in the best light possible. This isn't to say every trait is

redeemable—sometimes, people have annoying qualities—but the more we can ask this QBQ, "How can I accept and appreciate Harry for who he is?" the better we will work together.

Circle one: Agree   Disagree

Share any thoughts on why you chose to agree or disagree:

_____

_____

_____

3. Fill in the blank: "A _____ is someone who can look

   right _____ you and still enjoy the _____."

4. Whom do you need to be a friend like this for?

   Name: _____

   Do you have a friend like that? Name him or her: _____

   When and how will you contact this person and thank him

   or her for being such a good friend? Date: _____

   Form of communication: _____

CHAPTER TWENTY

Making Accountability Personal: All QBQs Contain an "I"

—| QBQ! |—

A corporate CEO projected "Personal Accountability begins with YOU!" on the screen. And yet, it begins with "me," not others. Personal accountability is just that—personal. It's all about the "I." Teams are important and groups are part of our world, but personal accountability is all about ME.

> ## Key Takeaway:
>
> **There is an "I" in "team"—and it's me!**

1. Quick review: The first QBQ guideline is:

   A QBQ begins with the words "What" or "_____."

   The second guideline:

   Every QBQ contains the personal pronoun "_____."

2. What makes it so tempting to believe or even say, "Personal accountability begins with YOU!" Record your thoughts:

_____

_____

_____

3. There are two myths of accountability:

   1. It's about holding others accountable.
   2. It's a team or group thing.

   Put an asterisk by the myth you've bought into the most.

4. A common belief, thought, and statement is "It's my job to hold them accountable." How does this way of thinking prevent us from practicing the QBQ! message of *personal* accountability?

_____

_____

_____

5. There is an "I" in "team"! Circle One: Agree   Disagree   Why?

_____

_____

_____

6. List three dangers in replacing the "I" in a QBQ with "we".

_____

_____

_____

7. Have you been involved in an "accountability group" or had an "accountability partner"? What were the benefits? Any negatives?

_____

_____

_____

8. The guideline of the QBQ always containing an "I" is the most difficult of the three QBQ guidelines to adhere to. Why is that?

_____

_____

_____

CHAPTER TWENTY-ONE

I Can Only Change Me

$=\boxed{\text{QBQ!}}=$

A vice president invested in a training program to fix just one employee. Some people think it's their job to change others, and lots of people have lots of ideas about what to change to improve their organization. Rarely, though, does anyone just say, "Today I will change me and that'll improve the organization!"

Key Takeaway:

The only person I can change is myself.

1. Have you been picturing someone who you wish would

   change? Write that person's name here: _____

2. In what ways have you tried to "fix" this person? How have
   your attempts affected the relationship?

   _____

   _____

   _____

3. What's the ONE thing you'd change to enhance the effectiveness

   of your _____ (organization, work, home, family—fill in

   the blank with what applies to you)? The one thing I'd change is:

   _____

4. Fill in the blank: "The bottom line is that the QBQ works

   because it's based on the truth *I can only change* _____!"

   Do you agree with this? Is it a true statement? Why or why not?

   _____

   _____

   _____

5. Circle below the things you have control over:

the weather   my child's choices

my finances   my spouse

my attitude   my employer

my child's attitude   my job

my choices   my teammates

6. What have you been trying to control that you will now let go of?

_____

7. List three to five things about an organization you're involved with that you'd like to see change.

_____

_____

_____

What would changing *you* do to contribute to what you've identified above?

_____

_____

_____

8. Everyone falls into the trap of trying to change someone else. Managers, parents, siblings, friends, work colleagues.

In which role listed above do you struggle the most to let people be who they are?

_____

CHAPTER TWENTY-TWO

"He Didn't, I Did"

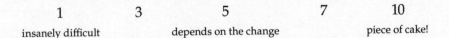

A branch manager overseeing a certain employee for a second time in a new office discovered that when she stopped trying to change the employee and instead changed herself, everything was better.

Key Takeaway:

Everything is better when I work to change myself.

1. On a scale of 1 to 10, changing myself is

1	3	5	7	10
insanely difficult		depends on the change		piece of cake!

2. Reflect on your past. What was a flaw or weakness you had that you were able to identify and correct? How did you overcome it? In what ways did you change?

_____

_____

_____

_____

_____

3. When a branch manager at Jostens realized she was trying to change her employee, and *that's* what was making their working relationship difficult, she decided to make a change. And that change didn't involve the other person; it involved only herself. When asked how the improvement in their relationship occurred, she made this key statement: "I stopped trying to change him."

Do you have someone in your life whom you stopped trying to

change? Name that person here: _____

What did this change in you do for the relationship?

_____

_____

_____

4. What are three ways you'd like to change yourself?

I would like to change _____.

I would like to change _____.

I would like to change _____.

CALL TO ACTION

What is the most important idea for me to apply from chapters 19–22?

_____

_____

_____

What steps will I take to make this change? When will I start? Be as specific as possible.

_____

_____

_____

How will my life improve by taking this action?

_____

_____

_____

CHAPTER TWENTY-THREE

"When Will Others Walk Their Talk?"

—[QBQ!]—

There are many ways people's actions don't match their words, and it's often easy to spot those gaps. People of integrity, though, work hard to make sure they live according to their stated beliefs. It doesn't matter what everyone else is doing or not doing. Walking our own talk first is job one.

Key Takeaway:

Accountable people focus on walking their own talk.

1. "Careful. The easiest thing to spot is gaps of integrity in others."

   Circle one: Agree   Disagree

   What "integrity gaps" do you tend to see in others immediately?

   _____

   _____

   _____

2. Of the following words, my top three values are (circle three):

   integrity   accountability

   authenticity   ownership

   kindness   creativity

   inclusivity   service

   trust   _____

   Are you currently living life in line with the values you circled above? Where are you struggling the most?

   _____

   _____

   _____

3. The definition of integrity:

   "Being what I _____ I am by acting in accordance

   with my _____."

   Am I living a life of integrity? Circle one: Yes! No! Trying to!

4. Here's an example of an IQ (incorrect question): "When will others walk their talk?" The better question to ask is a QBQ, like "How can I practice the principles I espouse?"

   Write out an answer to the QBQ above.

   _____

   _____

   _____

CHAPTER TWENTY-FOUR

An Integrity Test

—[QBQ!]—

The difference between having a "job" and having a "career" is one's level of belief in the organization, its goals, its people, and one's own ability to accomplish tasks. The QBQ "integrity test" is about making sure what is said at home about our organization matches what is said at work. If that test is failed, risk taking may be needed. We may need to find somewhere else to be employed. Life is too short to not believe in the entity we represent.

> ### Key Takeaway:
>
> **Life is too short to do something
> I don't believe in.**

1. The integrity test:

   "Does what I say about my organization while I'm at work match what I say at home?"

Be honest—did you pass? Circle one: Yes   No   How so?

_____

_____

_____

2. The idea of "believe or leave" can be a tough one for some
   folks, but it's an essential piece of personal growth and success
   on the job. If you believe in what you're doing, and the company you work for, and the people you work with, your ability
   to embrace change, solve problems, and coach others is enhanced. If you don't believe in what you're doing, perhaps it's
   time to leave and find something worth believing in. What is
   your response to the concept of "believe or leave"? How does it
   make you feel?

_____

_____

_____

3. Belief in your organization, its mission, its values, and what it stands for in the marketplace is important. With 1 representing low and 5 representing high, rate your level of belief in your organization: _____.

No matter what number rating you gave your level of belief, ask the QBQ "What can I do to build my belief?" Answer that QBQ below.

_____

_____

_____

4. Is your organization a vehicle to help you reach your personal goals? If so, how does it do so?

_____

_____

_____

5. Whatever your role or position is, is it a good fit for you? How are your personal goals being fulfilled through your position? Reflect and write your thoughts below.

_____

_____

_____

6. Is it time for you to leave? If so, why? What's missing that makes you want to leave?

_____

_____

_____

CHAPTER TWENTY-FIVE

The Power of One

—=[QBQ!]=—

"Hiding behind the team" means using the team and team-mates as excuses for goals not being achieved, project deadlines not being met, and results not being obtained. It's easy to do but detrimental in so many ways. Accountable people understand the power of one. They realize that the team is more functional when each individual practices personal accountability.

> **Key Takeaway:**
>
> **Accountable people don't hide behind the team.**

1. Circle the correct word to complete the sentence: QBQs always

   contain the word _____.

   "we"   "us"   "you"   "I"

2. It's easy to hide behind the team by saying . . .

"The team didn't meet the deadline."
"The team wasn't given enough resources."
"The team didn't get the job done."
"The team didn't have a clear mission."

How do these statements keep you from practicing personal accountability?

_____

_____

_____

3. How have you hidden behind the team? Have you ever used "the team" as an excuse for goals not being achieved? Give examples.

_____

_____

_____

4. Fill in the blank: "_____ accountability is not

about changing _____. It's about making a

_____ by changing _____."

5. The "power of one" idea speaks to the impact that ONE individual can make. It's not to say teams can't be impactful, but
the team is so much *more* efficient and strong when each *indi-*
vidual focuses on himself and believes in the power of one. If
you believe in the "power of one" concept, how will *you* now
handle a difficult situation in your life? Be specific.

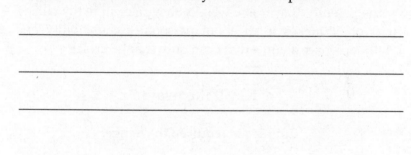

CHAPTER TWENTY-SIX

A QBQ Twist

The Serenity Prayer is a well-known piece in many circles. A twist on it makes it all about personal accountability and a reminder—once again—that I can only change myself.

Key Takeaway:

Courage is required to change.

1. What does serenity mean to you? Describe it in your own words.

_____

_____

_____

2. Do you feel like a person of courage? Why or why not?

   _____

   _____

   _____

3. What is one thing in your life you believe you cannot change
   and you must let go of?

   _____

   _____

   _____

4. Do you have the courage to do so? If not, here's a QBQ to reflect
   on: "What can I do to increase my courage?"

   _____

   _____

   _____

CHAPTER TWENTY-SEVEN

Will the Real Role Models Please Stand Up!

—|QBQ!|—

Everyone has the chance to be a role model. In fact, we are all role models because we all have someone watching us. Saying someone else is the role model and being disappointed when he or she falls from grace is actually a form of blame. Accountable individuals take their role model responsibility seriously.

> ### Key Takeaway:
>
> **Modeling is the most powerful of all teachers.**

1. Who were your role models in the past?

_____

_____

_____

2. Whom are you a role model for now?

_____

_____

_____

3. What good and what poor behaviors have you been modeling?

_____

_____

_____

4. Name your current mentors and describe what they've done and continue to do for you.

_____

_____

_____

5. Why is modeling "the most powerful teacher"?

_____

_____

_____

CALL TO ACTION

What is the most important idea for me to apply from chapters
23–27?

_____

_____

_____

What steps will I take to make this change? When will I start?
Be as specific as possible.

_____

_____

_____

How will my life improve by taking this action?

_____

_____

_____

CHAPTER TWENTY-EIGHT

Practicing Personal Accountability: All QBQs Focus on Action

=| QBQ! |=

While in a training session, hearing about QBQ for the first time, a middle manager realized he needed to take action—immediately. So he slipped out of the meeting briefly and arranged travel back to the headquarters so he could solve a problem. It is through action that things get accomplished. Without action, there is no forward progress, no solution, no success. The third guideline to creating a QBQ is it must focus on action.

Key Takeaway:

Accountable people take action.

1. What problems have you been griping and complaining about?

   _____

   _____

   _____

2. The middle manager succeeded because he changed his thinking. He stopped complaining, asked better questions, and took
   action! How would doing any or all of these three steps benefit
   you in moving past the problems you listed above?

   _____

   _____

   _____

3. What is one action you will take now—as soon as possible—to
   solve a problem identified in question No. 1?

   _____

   _____

   _____

4. Review! The three QBQ guidelines:

Every QBQ begins with "W_____" or "H_____."

Every QBQ contains an "_____."

Every QBQ focuses on "_____."

5. Identify three emotional benefits to taking action and getting stuff done.

_____

_____

_____

CHAPTER TWENTY-NINE

The Risk of Doing Nothing

—[QBQ!]—

A senior executive gives advice on the importance of taking risk. And action. Action is always better than inaction, even if the course must later change. Taking action—which often entails risk and sometimes making mistakes—is almost always a good idea. Some people need to be told to wait, but others wait to be told, which rarely adds value to our organizations and our lives.

Key Takeaway:

Action beats inaction and has many benefits.

1. Simply put, what is the risk or the cost of "doing nothing"?

   _____

   _____

   _____

2. What does initiative mean to you? Do you have it? Be honest!

   _____

   _____

   _____

3. In what area of life do you need to bolster your initiative? Circle all that apply.

   my career   my long-term goals

   my spiritual life   my household management

   my relationships   my pursuit of dreams

   my parenting   Other: _____

   my financial management   Other: _____

   my physical health

4. Benefits of action:

- Action brings learning and growth.

- Action leads us toward solutions.

- Action requires courage.

- Action builds confidence.

- What can you add?

_____

_____

_____

5. "It's better to be one who is told to wait than one who waits to be told."

Circle one: Agree   Disagree   Why?

_____

_____

_____

6. Of the two options above, which side do you tend to err on? Which would you *rather* err on?

_____

_____

_____

7. Write down one thing you need to take action on *today*:

_____

CALL TO ACTION

What is the most important idea for me to apply from chapters 28–29?

_____

_____

_____

What steps will I take to make this change? When will I start? Be as specific as possible.

_____

_____

_____

How will my life improve by taking this action?

_____

_____

_____

CHAPTER THIRTY

"Thanks for Shopping at the Home Depot!"

— QBQ! —

A cashier at a home improvement retailer solved a customer's problem without complaining about her lack of resources, lack of quality systems, or lack of support. She went above and beyond and made an impact.

> ## Key Takeaway:
>
> ### One person can make a big impact.

1. Judy, the cashier at the home improvement store, had a choice to make in the moment. A customer had only a $100 bill to pay for less than $5 worth of product, and she didn't have the necessary change in her drawer to break the bill. In that moment, Judy made a choice. She did not ask these IQs:

   "Why don't I get more cash in the drawer?"
   "Why do we have to use the pneumatic tube process?"

"Why do I have to start so early in the morning?"
"When am I going to get more support?"
"Who's going to coach and mentor me?"
"Why can't the customer bring smaller bills?"
"Why are customers so demanding?"

Put an asterisk next to any of the above IQs that you admit you might have asked if you'd been in Judy's situation.

2. After considering the Home Depot story, how would you fill in the blanks?

QBQ: "What can I do to _____?"

QBQ: "How can I help _____ the problem?"

3. Project yourself into Judy's mind. When her customer rushed up to her to check out, imagine the QBQ that might've been in her mind. Now write it out. Remember, use the three QBQ guidelines. (Begins with "What" or "How," contains an "I," and focuses on "Action.")

_____

_____

_____

4. If you had been Judy's customer, how would you have felt about the Home Depot and Judy that day? If you would have

shared the experience with friends and family, what adjectives would you have used?

_____

_____

_____

5. What outstanding customer service experience have you had that Judy's story reminds you of? Describe it and then ask, "What can I do to take actions like these?"

_____

_____

_____

6. Describe a time *you* were Judy and did something to delight your customer.

_____

_____

_____

7. What would "going higher in life" look like to you? In what areas of life would you most like to make this happen?

_____

_____

_____

CHAPTER THIRTY-ONE

Leaders at All Levels

|QBQ!|

A man declared in jest that he was a leader because his name was "Jim Leader"! In reality, we are all leaders. Leadership is not about position, title, tenure, or loyalty. None of these are indicators of true leadership. Leadership, more than anything else, is about the way we think. It's a moment-to-moment disciplining of our thoughts. It is very much about the choices we make.

Key Takeaway:

**If you think like a leader,
you are a leader.**

1. What is leadership to me?

_____

_____

_____

2. Am I a leader? What are my leadership roles?

_____

_____

_____

3. How can leaders differ from each other?

_____

_____

_____

4. Why do people often believe that leadership is all about title, position, or tenure?

_____

_____

5. Where does parenting rank as a leadership role?

_____

_____

_____

6. How is being a friend an opportunity to lead?

_____

_____

7. Are people "born" leaders, or do we learn to lead?

_____

_____

8. What are three specific leadership skills people can learn/acquire?

_____

_____

_____

9. Why do so few people raise their hands to the question "How many of you are leaders?"

_____

_____

_____

10. "Leadership, more than anything else, is about the way we think. It's the moment-to-moment disciplining of our thoughts." What do you think about this definition of leadership?

_____

_____

_____

CHAPTER THIRTY-TWO

The Cornerstone of Leadership

QBQ!

In the chapter 1 story of Jacob the restaurant server, the restaurant manager, Jacob's supervisor, chose to serve her employee by leaving the premises to get the Diet Coke the customer had asked for, so that Jacob could go above and beyond for his customer. She didn't pull rank on him, check to see how well he was performing that month, or ask what he would then do for her. This shows her leadership skills. True leadership begins with humility, which is the cornerstone of leadership, as well as a servant's heart.

> ## Key Takeaway:
>
> **Humility is the cornerstone of leadership.**

1. If you have ever had a manager like Jacob's, jot down his or her name here:

_____

2. In what way(s) was this person like Jacob's manager? Be specific.

_____

_____

_____

3. Imagine and describe what Jacob's manager could have said to him when he asked her to go get the Diet Coke.

_____

_____

_____

4. In outstanding organizations, going the "extra mile" as Jacob and his manager did isn't just allowed, it's encouraged. Is this true in your organization? Reflect and record your thoughts.

_____

_____

_____

_____

5. When you see the phrase "servant leadership," what character traits come to mind?

_____

_____

_____

6. Are you a servant leader? How so?

_____

_____

_____

7. Humility is the cornerstone of leadership. How is this true?

_____

_____

_____

8. Picture a person you admire, one whom you're drawn to. List the traits this person exhibits.

_____

_____

_____

9. Name three people—friends, family, colleagues, public figures, professional athletes, celebrities—who you believe demonstrate humility.

_____

_____

_____

Note: To explore what outstanding organizations and people do differently, read *Outstanding! 47 Ways to Make Your Organization Exceptional* by John G. Miller.

CHAPTER THIRTY-THREE

Accountability and Boundaries

—=| QBQ! |=—

Practicing personal accountability is never about doing other people's work for them, cutting corners for them, or enabling them. Caring for and serving others are important, but not if boundaries are crossed. The individual who employs the QBQ and truly grasps personal accountability knows and understands the importance of setting appropriate boundaries.

Key Takeaway:

Accountable people concentrate on excelling in their own work.

1. Some people are tempted to do other people's work for them. I am tempted to do the work for

   my child   my friend

   my spouse   my family member

   my co-worker   Other: _____

2. How is it a disservice to others when we cover for them or do
   their work?

   _____

   _____

   _____

3. Honestly, whom have I done this to or am currently doing it to?

   _____

   Will I stop now? Circle one: Yes   No

4. Have you seen someone cover for or enable others? What negative results of this did you observe? What can you learn from
   seeing someone else make this mistake?

   _____

   _____

   _____

   _____

   _____

5. Share a time when you covered for other people and/or you crossed boundaries and enabled them. Who was it? Did it help or hurt in the long run?

_____

_____

_____

6. Honest assessment: On a scale of 1 to 10, how good are you at drawing healthy boundaries (1 is poor, 10 is excellent)?

_____

7. A great QBQ is "What can I do to maintain appropriate boundaries?" Name the people you need to draw better boundaries with.

_____

_____

_____

8. List the specific boundaries you need to establish with these people:

   (Example: I will not discuss my co-worker's marital woes with him anymore. Or, I will ask how I can help my second-in-command, but I will not complete the whole project for her.)

   _____

   _____

   _____

9. One of the most common situations where boundaries are crossed is in the parent-child relationship. If you're a mom or dad, how are you doing in this area?

   _____

   _____

   _____

Note: For more ideas on effective, accountable parenting, please read *Raising Accountable Kids: How to Be an Outstanding Parent Using the Power of Personal Accountability* by John G. Miller and Karen G. Miller.

CALL TO ACTION

What is the most important idea for me to apply from chapters 30–33?

_____

_____

_____

What steps will I take to make this change? When will I start? Be as specific as possible.

_____

_____

_____

How will my life improve by taking this action?

_____

_____

_____

CHAPTER THIRTY-FOUR

A Great List of Lousy Questions

—[QBQ!]—

There are many incorrect questions (IQs) commonly heard in the marketplace—from sales to customer service to management. We even hear them at home, at church, in our parenting, and with our neighbors and friends. No matter what these negative questions are or where they're asked, the better approach is always asking a QBQ.

> ## Key Takeaway:
>
> **I can ask incorrect questions or QBQs; the choice is always mine.**

For your convenience, we have included here all of the QBQs and IQs listed in the *QBQ!* book in chapter 34.

1. Write a *V* next to the questions that lead to Victim Thinking, a *P* next to the ones that result in Procrastination, and a *B* next to the ones that cause Blame.

2. Put an asterisk next to every IQ you admit that you've asked yourself.

CUSTOMER SERVICE IQs:

"When will shipping start getting orders out on time?"
"Why does the customer expect so much?"
"When will the sales department do it right the first time?"

QBQ:

"How can I serve them?"

SALES IQs:

"Why are our prices so high?"
"When are we going to be more competitive?"
"Why won't the customer call me back?"
"When will marketing give us better materials?"
"Why can't manufacturing make what we sell?"

QBQs:

"What can I do today to be more effective?"
"How can I add value for my customers?"

OPERATIONS OR MANUFACTURING IQs:

"Why can't sales just sell what we make?"
"When will they learn to sell the right specs?"
"Who's going to get them to understand?"

QBQs:

"How can I better understand the challenges faced by the field?"
"What can I do to build rapport with the salespeople?"

Management IQs:

"Why doesn't the younger generation want to work?"
"When will we find good people?"
"Why aren't they motivated?"
"Who made the mistake?"
"Why can't people come in on time?"
"When will they get engaged?"

QBQs:

"How can I be a more effective coach?"
"What can I do to better understand each person I manage?"
"How can I build a stronger team?"

Executive IQs:

"Who dropped the ball?"
"When are they going to catch the vision?"
"Who's going to care as much as I do?"
"When will the market turn around?"

QBQs:

"How can I be a better leader?"
"What can I do to show I care?"
"How can I communicate more effectively?"

EMPLOYEE IQs:

"Why do we have to go through all this change?"
"When is someone going to train me?"
"Why don't I get paid more?"
"Who's going to clarify my job?"
"When is management going to get their act together?"
"Who's going to give us the vision?"

QBQs:

"What can I do to be more productive?"
"How can I adapt to the changing environment?"
"What can I do to develop myself?"
"How can I become more engaged?"

MARKETING IQs:

"When will the salespeople deliver our programs?"
"Why won't the field learn more about our new products?"
"When is someone going to listen to us?"

QBQs:

"What can I do to understand the sales reps' frustrations?"
"How can I learn more about what the customer wants?"
"What can I do to articulate my ideas more creatively?"

And from the world outside work . . .

STUDENT IQs:

"Why doesn't my teacher understand me?"
"When will my parents support me more?"
"Who's going to help me improve my grades?"

QBQs:

"How can I focus more effectively?"
"What can I do to form good study habits?"
"How can I own my grades?"

Note: If you would like to share the QBQ message of personal account-ability with youth, acquire the high/middle school classroom curriculum *I Own It! Building Character Through Personal Accountability*, created by Kristin E. Lindeen.

TEACHER IQs:

"Why aren't parents more involved?"
"When will the kids start caring more?"
"Who will find me better students?"
"Why am I so overworked and underpaid?"

QBQs:

"How can I better support each of the kids in my classroom?"
"What can I do to own the performance of my students?"
"How can I be more creative in my instruction?"
"What can I do to rediscover my passion for teaching?"

PARENT IQs:

"When is my child going to listen to me?"
"Why does my daughter hang out with those kids?"
"When will my son open up to me?"
"Who made the mess in here?"
"Why can't you be more like your sister?"

QBQs:

"How can I get to know him better?"
"What can I do to help her get through these tough years?"
"How can I improve my parenting skills?"

TEENAGER IQs:

"When are my parents going to 'get it'?"
"Why don't they like my friends?"
"Who's going to give me a job?"
"When will I find time to get everything done?"

QBQs:

"How can I show more respect to Mom and Dad?"
"What can I do to communicate better?"
"How can I manage my time more effectively?"

Note: To learn how to apply the QBQ message of personal accountability at home, read *Raising Accountable Kids: How to Be an Outstanding Parent Using the Power of Personal Accountability* by John G. Miller and Karen G. Miller.

SPOUSE/PARTNER IQs:

"Why doesn't he let go of that old issue?"
"When will she appreciate me more?"
"Why don't you start exercising?"

QBQs:

"How can I improve myself today?"
"What can I do to help her out?"
"How can I listen to him more?"

NEIGHBOR IQ:

"Why are they so unfriendly?"

QBQ:

"How can I be a better friend?"

Volunteer IQs:

"Why do I have to do everything myself?"
"When will other people start helping out?"

QBQ:

"What can I do to set better boundaries and just say no?"

3. Identify three to five of the QBQs from the examples given that
   you plan to ask today. List them here:

   _____

   _____

   _____

CHAPTER THIRTY-FIVE

The Spirit of the QBQ

—|QBQ!|—

In addition to the three guidelines for creating a QBQ, there's a spirit to The Question Behind the Question. QBQs carry a message and tone of humility, service, accountability, and ownership and, of course, a recognition that we can only change ourselves. Individuals can build and ask QBQs that meet the guidelines, but do they have the spirit? If not, this is not personal accountability.

> **Key Takeaway:**
>
> **Understanding the spirit of the QBQ
> is as important as using the three guidelines.**

1. Reflect on the ideas and principles underlying every QBQ, and list five or more words that might describe the QBQ spirit.

_____

_____

_____

2. Are you more of a letter of the law or a spirit of the law person? Jot down examples below.

_____

_____

_____

3. For fun, create some questions that meet the three QBQ guidelines but lack the spirit! (Reminder, the QBQ guidelines: QBQs begin with "What" or "How," contain an "I," and focus on "Action.")

Examples of a question that meets the guidelines but lacks the spirit: "What can I do to make you change?" "How can I avoid responsibility right now?"

_____

_____

_____

4. One example of a question that adheres to the guidelines but lacks the spirit is "Who can I blame today?" In reality, that's a pretty common question in today's world. Share a time you asked that question. What was the situation? Why is it so tempting to ask it? Reflect and write.

_____

_____

_____

CHAPTER THIRTY-SIX

Wisdom

—[QBQ!]—

Wisdom is not complicated. It's actually quite simple. Its basis is recognizing that nobody ever fully arrives, and if we ever believe we know everything there is to know, we're dead wrong. Living a life of personal accountability, learning, and being our personal best is a lifelong journey.

> ### Key Takeaway:
>
> **No one is a finished product.**

1. "Wisdom: what we learn after we know it all." Reflect on what it takes to gain wisdom. List three practical first steps to becoming a wiser person.

_____

_____

_____

2. Describe a person who thinks he's "arrived." Now describe one who knows he's not a finished product. What stands out as the key difference or differences? Which person are you?

_____

_____

_____

3. What specific area of your life comes to mind where you need to continue the learning journey? Record three action steps you'll take toward more learning.

_____

_____

_____

4. How will asking QBQs help you gain more wisdom and live by it?

_____

_____

_____

CHAPTER THIRTY-SEVEN

We Buy Too Many Books

—| QBQ! |—

Many people attend seminars and buy books simply because they like to attend seminars and own new books! We may even listen attentively and read in a studious fashion. But it's all a waste if we don't change. When we really change, we've really learned. Learning isn't acquiring knowledge, buying books, or ingesting information. Learning equals change!

Key Takeaway:

If I haven't changed, I haven't learned.

1. We buy too many books and attend too many seminars without really ever making a change. Do you agree or disagree? Why or why not?

_____

_____

_____

2. Learning equals (check all that apply)

    ❑ listening   ❑ gaining knowledge
    ❑ showing up   ❑ changing
    ❑ reading   ❑ proclaiming "Amen!"
    ❑ attending   ❑ knowing
    ❑ nodding my head

3. What are the dangers of believing we've "learned" just because we attended a seminar or class or read a book?

4. What is the danger in gaining knowledge, but never changing?

5. What is the value in making a behavioral change—that is, acting on new knowledge?

   _____

   _____

   _____

6. While exploring *QBQ!* material, what have you learned about
   yourself? How, if at all, have you changed?

   _____

   _____

   _____

CHAPTER THIRTY-EIGHT

A Final Picture

QBQ!

A sidewalk-cruising, wheelchair-bound man dove from his chair to the ground. He then began to crawl, reaching for newspapers blowing in the wind, clutching them to his chest. This scene caught the attention of a family driving by. Stopping and helping him, they learned about personal accountability. The man took complete ownership for his "mess" and taught a powerful lesson in doing so. Believing and saying, "It's my mess," and then taking action to solve the problem is a powerful example of what QBQ stands for. No Blame, Victim Thinking, or Procrastination—just asking QBQs such as "What can I do?" and "How can I help?"

Key Takeaway:

**Personal accountability and QBQ
are needed in our organizations and our lives.**

1. What feelings did the story of Brian in the wheelchair evoke in you?

   _____

   _____

   _____

2. Did Brian take too much responsibility for the newspapers? What else could he have done? What would you have done? Reflect and write.

   _____

   _____

   _____

3. Brian is an exemplar of the concept of ownership. What "mess" in your life do you need to own? Some examples:

   "My department is not as productive as it could be . . .
   It's my mess!"
   "My relationships aren't what I want them to be . . .
   It's my mess!"
   "My team isn't gelling the way I wish it would . . .
   It's my mess!"
   "My life isn't turning out the way I thought . . .
   It's my mess!"

Jot down a mess or two you will own *today*.

_____

_____

_____

4. There are many stories throughout the *QBQ!* book, and each has its own way of illustrating personal accountability.

Stacey and her pilot dad show how important it is to say, "How can I adapt to the changing world?" while Bonita and her Santa Claus cap remind us to say, "How can I make a difference?" even when the situation is tough.

Jacob and the Diet Coke story is all about saying, "What can I do to serve?" and Judy helps show the power of one by asking, "How can I achieve with the resources I have?"

And of course, Brian with his newspapers teaches us the importance of ownership and asking, "What can I do to own this mess?"

Underline the QBQs above, and choose the one you need to apply most and write it below:

_____

5. Of all the stories in the *QBQ!* book, including the five listed in
   question 4., which one is your favorite and why?

   _____

   _____

   _____

6. "If more people practiced personal accountability, the world
   would be a better place."

   As you begin to practice more personal accountability using
   the QBQ, how will *your* world improve? List the positive
   changes you will work to achieve.

   _____

   _____

   _____

CHAPTER THIRTY-NINE

The Motor of Learning

QBQ!

The Secret to Learning Is Repetition

Key Takeaway:

There is power in repetition.

1. What causes you to fail to return to an idea or topic you've learned about? Let's say you attend a seminar and take a bunch of notes. What might cause you to never refer back to those notes to reinforce the content in your mind?

_____

_____

_____

2. In many organizations, training is a onetime thing or event. Why is that, and what are the costs?

_____

_____

_____

3. List three consequences of being exposed to an idea only once.

_____

_____

_____

4. How will you repeat and reinforce the *QBQ!* message?

_____

_____

_____

5. How many times have you read the *QBQ!* book? Will you read it again? Be honest!

_____

_____

_____

6. If you've read *QBQ!* more than once, list the ideas that jumped out at you this time versus your first reading.

_____

_____

_____

7. Consider how you will apply the principles and ideas you've worked through in this workbook now that you've completed it. Write down your plan.

_____

_____

_____

CALL TO ACTION

What is the most important idea for me to apply from chapters 34–39?

_____

_____

_____

What steps will I take to make this change? When will I start? Be as specific as possible.

_____

_____

_____

How will my life improve by taking this action?

_____

_____

_____

Before We Go

We'd like to direct your attention to the FAQs at the end of the book *QBQ! The Question Behind the Question*. These relevant, insightful questions come from clients of QBQ, Inc. who experienced the QBQ training program in-house, attended a live QBQ event, or read the *QBQ!* book. We recommend that you read and ponder each one. Considering these questions will provide even greater clarity for you around what the QBQ is, how to utilize it, and how it can and will add value to your life!

VISIT QBQ.COM TO LEARN ABOUT:

- The easy-to-use multimedia training system *Personal Accountability and the QBQ!* designed to be implemented in-house by your facilitators.
- Securing author John G. Miller or Kristin E. Lindeen to speak at your organization, conference, or event.
- *Flipping the Switch*, the companion book to *QBQ!* that takes the QBQ to the next level.
- *Outstanding! 47 Ways to Make Your Organization Exceptional*, the book that enables organizations to excel.
- *Raising Accountable Kids* by John G. Miller and Karen G. Miller, written to help parents raise a generation of responsible adults.

QBQ, Inc., Denver, Colorado, 303-286-9900, Info@QBQ.com, QBQ.com

Helping Organizations Make Personal Accountability a Core Value

About the Authors
of *The QBQ! Workbook*

JOHN G. MILLER is the author of *QBQ! The Question Behind the Question, Flipping the Switch: Unleash the Power of Personal Accountability Using the QBQ!,* and *Outstanding! 47 Ways to Make Your Organization Exceptional.* He is the founder of QBQ, Inc., an organizational development firm based in Colorado dedicated to *Helping Organizations Make Personal Accountability a Core Value.* A 1980 graduate of Cornell University, John has been involved in the training and speaking industry since 1986. He lives in Denver with his wife, Karen. Together, John and Karen authored *Raising Accountable Kids: How to Be an Outstanding Parent Using the Power of Personal Accountability.* They have seven children and an ever growing number of grandchildren. E-mail John at John@QBQ.com.

KRISTIN E. LINDEEN grew up in the home of *QBQ!* as the oldest of seven Miller children. Steeped in the QBQ message of personal accountability, she is uniquely equipped to share it with others. She is a keynote speaker and workshop leader whose clients range from large corporations to rural associations, public and private schools, churches, and nonprofits. Kristin holds an M.A. in curriculum design from Colorado Christian University and enjoys delivering practical content with an energetic and fun style. She is also the creator of *I Own It! Building Character Through Personal Accountability*—a classroom curriculum for schools. Kristin lives in Maple Grove, Minnesota, with her husband, Erik, and their children, Joshua, Rebecca, and Andrew. E-mail her at Kristin@QBQ.com.

Helping businesses, organizations, and families make personal accountability a core value.

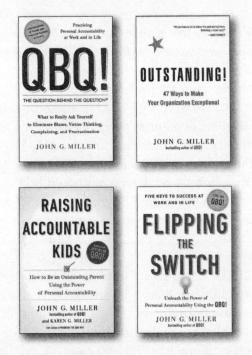

Most Penguin Random House LLC books are available at special quantity discounts for bulk purchases for sales promotions, premiums, fundraising, or educational use. Customized books or book excerpts can be created to fit specific needs.

To order bulk copies for giveaways, premiums, distribution to employees, sales promotions, or education, contact:

Penguin Random House Premium Sales
Phone: 212.572.2232 | Fax: 212.366.2679
specialmarkets@penguinrandomhouse.com
www.penguinrandomhouse.biz/specialmarkets/premium